Using Simple Machines

Screws All Around

by Trudy Becker

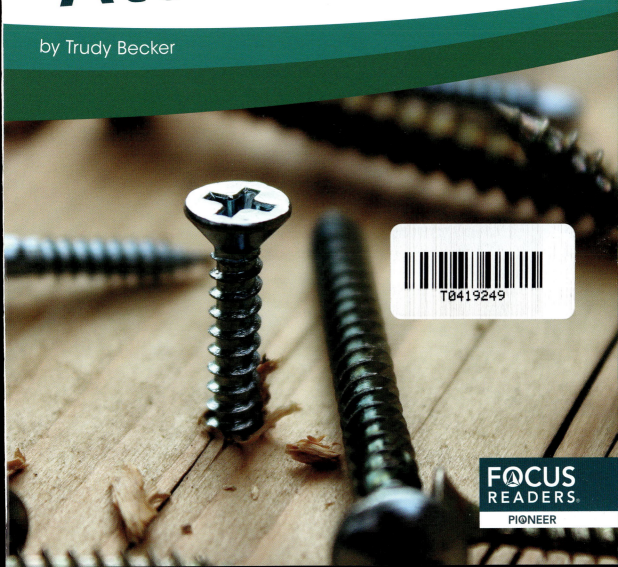

FOCUS READERS.
PIONEER

www.focusreaders.com

Copyright © 2024 by Focus Readers®, Lake Elmo, MN 55042. All rights reserved. No part of this book may be reproduced or utilized in any form or by any means without written permission from the publisher.

Focus Readers is distributed by North Star Editions:
sales@northstareditions.com | 888-417-0195

Produced for Focus Readers by Red Line Editorial.

Photographs ©: Shutterstock Images, cover, 1, 4, 8, 10, 14, 17, 20; iStockphoto, 6, 12 (top), 12 (bottom), 18

Library of Congress Cataloging-in-Publication Data
Names: Becker, Trudy, author.
Title: Screws all around / by Trudy Becker.
Description: Lake Elmo, MN : Focus Readers, [2024] | Series: Using simple machines | Includes bibliographical references and index. | Audience: Grades K-1
Identifiers: LCCN 2022059426 (print) | LCCN 2022059427 (ebook) | ISBN 9781637396001 (hardcover) | ISBN 9781637396575 (paperback) | ISBN 9781637397695 (ebook pdf) | ISBN 9781637397145 (hosted ebook)
Subjects: LCSH: Screws--Juvenile literature.
Classification: LCC TJ1338 .B345 2024 (print) | LCC TJ1338 (ebook) | DDC 621.8/82--dc23/eng/20230103
LC record available at https://lccn.loc.gov/2022059426
LC ebook record available at https://lccn.loc.gov/2022059427

Printed in the United States of America
Mankato, MN
082023

About the Author

Trudy Becker lives in Minneapolis, Minnesota. She likes exploring new places and loves anything involving books.

Table of Contents

CHAPTER 1
Turning Screws 5

CHAPTER 2
What Are Screws? 9

CHAPTER 3
Screws Everywhere 13

THAT'S AMAZING!
Ice Fishing 16

CHAPTER 4
Fun with Screws 19

Focus on Screws • 22
Glossary • 23
To Learn More • 24
Index • 24

Chapter 1

Turning Screws

A girl is building a desk. She picks up a screw. Then she gets a **screwdriver**. She holds the screw in place and turns the screwdriver. The screw pushes in. It holds the wood together.

Screws work by turning. Turning makes a screw push or move something. Screws have many uses. They are one of the six **simple machines**.

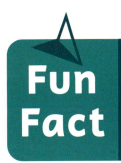

Fun Fact

Light bulbs use screws. People twist the bulbs into place.

Chapter 2

What Are Screws?

All simple machines help people do jobs. People can use screws to hold things together. Screws can also squeeze things. They can even help move or lift things.

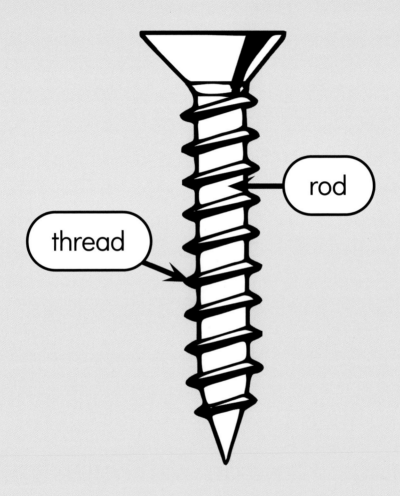

A screw has two parts. The center part is called the rod. The other part is the **thread**. The thread wraps around the rod. It makes a **spiral** shape.

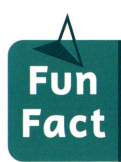

Fun Fact The thread of a screw is a twisted inclined plane.

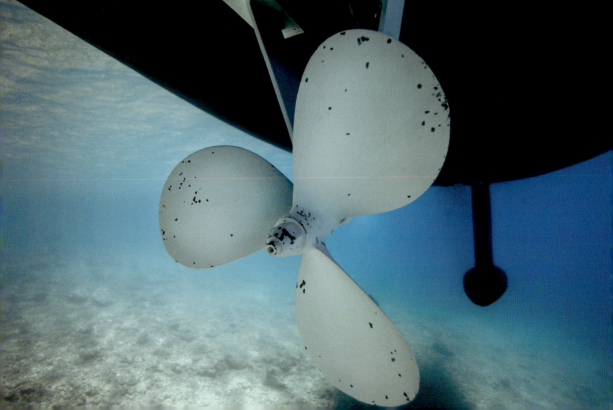

Chapter 3

Screws Everywhere

Screws are all around. Many bottles use screws to open and close. When the cap is turned, the screw pulls the pieces together. **Propellers** are screws, too. They move water when they turn.

A fan's **blades** work like a screw. The blades are inclined planes. They are attached to a rod. When the blades turn, they move the air. That helps people stay cool.

Fun Fact: The spiral shape of a screw helps it move through things. It turns a small **force** into a larger one.

That's Amazing!

Ice Fishing

People can use screws for ice fishing. They use **augers**. Fishers hold augers against the ice. Then they turn the augers. The augers break into the ice and go down. That makes holes. Fishers keep turning to go deeper. Then they can fish!

Chapter 4

Fun with Screws

People use screws for fun things, too. Water hoses have screws. People turn the **faucets**. That makes water start or stop flowing. People can water gardens or play in the water.

Some machines use screws to make juice. People put fruit in. Then they turn a screw. That makes the machine push on the fruit. It squeezes the juice out. Then people can drink.

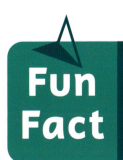

Fun Fact

Screws are used to build many toys.

FOCUS ON
Screws

Write your answers on a separate piece of paper.

1. Write a sentence that explains the main idea of Chapter 4.

2. What is the most helpful way you use screws in your life? Why?

3. What is the spiral part of a screw called?
- **A.** a rod
- **B.** a thread
- **C.** a propeller

4. Why might someone want to use a machine with a screw to help make fruit juice?
- **A.** It takes less force than squeezing by hand.
- **B.** It costs more than squeezing by hand.
- **C.** The juice tastes better that way.

Answer key on page 24.

Glossary

augers
Tools with spiral parts for drilling into things.

blades
The flat, wide parts of fans that spin.

faucets
Things that control the flow of water.

force
A push or pull that changes how something moves.

inclined plane
A ramp. It is one of the six simple machines.

propellers
Sets of spinning blades that help boats move.

screwdriver
A tool used to turn screws.

simple machines
Machines with only a few parts that make work easier.

spiral
A line that makes a curving, circular pattern.

thread
The spiral part of a screw that wraps around the center.

To Learn More

BOOKS

Blevins, Wiley. *Let's Find Screws*. North Mankato, MN: Capstone Press, 2021.

Mattern, Joanne. *Screws*. Minneapolis: Bellwether Media, 2020.

NOTE TO EDUCATORS

Visit **www.focusreaders.com** to find lesson plans, activities, links, and other resources related to this title.

Index

A
augers, 16

L
light bulbs, 7

S
screwdriver, 5

T
thread, 10–11

Answer Key: **1.** Answers will vary; **2.** Answers will vary; **3.** B; **4.** A